·SUPERBOOK

AMAZING FACTS

GEORGE BEAL

Kingfisher Books

Contents

Amazing Facts:
About People	4	About Food and Drink	24
About Places	8	About Inventions and Discoveries	26
About Buildings and Other Structures	10	About Entertainment	30
About the World and the Universe	14	About Language, Literature and Art	32
About Animals	16	About Sport	34
About Plants	20	About Things the World Over	38

Kingfisher Books, Grisewood & Dempsey Ltd,
Elsley House, 24–30 Great Titchfield Street,
London W1P 7AD

First published in 1986 by Kingfisher Books

Reprinted 1988, 1992 (with revisions)

Copyright © Grisewood & Dempsey 1986
All rights reserved. No part of this publication may be reproduced, stored in a retrieval system or transmitted by any means, electronic, mechanical, photocopying or otherwise, without the prior permission of the publisher.

BRITISH LIBRARY CATALOGUING IN PUBLICATION DATA
Beal, George
  Amazing Facts.
  1. Curiosities and wonders – Juvenile literature
  I. Title
  032'.02   AG243

ISBN 0-86272-202-0

Cover design by Terry Woodley
Cover illustration by Mike Saunders, Jillian Burgess Illustrations
Phototypeset by Southern Positives and Negatives (SPAN), Lingfield, Surrey
Printed in Hong Kong
Drawings by Paul Dowling

Previous page: some early American trains used sails to propel them – see page 28.

Opposite page: the flying frog from Costa Rica has feet like parachutes, which help it glide through the air.

Amazing Facts

Did you know that the only animal related to the mighty elephant is a tiny creature called a hyrax? That certain people consider the world's most poisonous fish a great delicacy? Or that in 1912 an airman called F. K. McClean got into trouble with the police when he flew his biplane under all the bridges between Tower Bridge and Westminster in London? This book is full of facts like these; facts to surprise you, facts to entertain you, facts you may find useful and facts you may not believe. There are amazing facts about familiar things (did you know that the Incas of South America ate popcorn?), and facts about things you certainly won't recognise. All sorts of people and all sorts of subjects are included – so whether it's sport or wildlife, machines or sea creatures, writers, radio broadcasts or the weather, or just about anything else that interests you, this book will amuse, amaze and entertain you.

About People

When a mysterious man called George Rex arrived in the Cape of Good Hope in 1795, he was treated with great respect. His name led people to believe that he was King George III of England.

Albert Einstein's last words were spoken in German. Nobody will ever know what they were, because his nurse spoke no German.

In 1937 the Maharajah of the Indian state of Bikaner was weighed on a scale against blocks of gold. The gold was then distributed to charities.

The figure of Britannia, which has appeared on British coins since 1665, is a portrait of a real person: Frances Stewart, later Duchess of Richmond. The original engraving was made by Philip Roetier.

▲ At the age of 30, Al Capone had been in control of organized crime in Chicago for four years, and his income had reached $5,000,000. He was finally gaoled for not paying his taxes.

Just before he was hanged for robbery and murder, the Australian outlaw Ned Kelly's last words were: 'Such is life'.

Hiroo Onoda, a Japanese soldier sent to a Philippine island during the Second World War, was unaware that the war had ended until a tourist told him in 1974.

Cleopatra, queen of Egypt in ancient times, was not Egyptian at all, but of pure Greek descent.

Slaves in ancient Rome had a life expectancy of only $17\frac{1}{2}$ years.

◀ The notorious highwayman Claude Duval used to enjoy a dance with any ladies travelling in the coaches he held up!

'Spring-heeled Jack' was a man who adopted bizarre disguises and terrorized the suburbs of London in 1837 and 1838. He made huge leaps in the air, and was seen as a 'large white bull', a 'white bear' and 'clad in brass armour, with large, claw-like gloves'. He was never caught.

A lady from Middlesex, England, gained her driving licence in 1987 – after a record 48 attempts and over 330 lessons!

King George I of England was unable to speak English – because he was German.

During the 9th century, the Danes occupying Ireland started a 'nose tax' of one ounce of gold per household. Non-payers had their noses slit.

Dr James Barry, a general in the British Army Medical Corps, was a woman – but this was not discovered until she died in 1865.

Deeds of Daring

In April 1986, two men lept from the top of the Empire State Building – on parachutes! Both landed safely in the street where one escaped in a taxi, and the other was arrested.

Windsurfers have ventured as far north as Greenland, south around Cape Horn, and one has circumnavigated the British Isles.

In 1977 George Willig, the 'human fly', climbed the outside of the 110-storey World Trade Centre in New York.

An English 'dangerous sports club' has performed a number of foolhardy pranks, including jumping from the Golden Gate suspension bridge in San Francisco on elasticated ropes!

◀ **Steve McPeak of the USA demonstrates his mastery of high-wire walking by climbing the cable which carries the cable car up the Sugar Loaf Mountain in Rio de Janeiro, Brazil.**

The first man to fly under Westminster Bridge in London was F. K. McClean, who also flew between the upper and lower parts of Tower Bridge, and all the bridges in between, in 1912. When he landed on the river at Westminster, he was instructed by the police to 'move along'. Unfortunately, the plane was damaged during take-off, and had to be removed by road.

The Roman emperor Caligula's real name was Gaius Julius Caesar Germanicus – Caligula was a nickname that meant 'little boots'. One of the mad emperor's more bizarre decrees was that his favourite horse, Incitatus, be made a consul of Rome.

Mustapha Kemal, who became leader of Turkey in 1922, adopted the name 'Ataturk', which means 'father of the Turks'. 'Kemal' means 'perfection'.

◀ In 1971, 29 students from a London college managed to stand on top of a Post Office pillar box.

The Biggest

The tallest recorded human being was Robert Wadlow, who died in the USA at the age of 22 having reached 2.72 m (8 ft 11 in) in height. The tallest groups of people in the world are found in central Africa, where the average height of some tribes exceeds 1.83 m (6 ft).

Captain William Bligh didn't only have trouble as captain of the ship *Bounty*. When he became governor of New South Wales in Australia, local army officers rebelled against him.

Jean Gabrielle Peltier, a French journalist and refugee in London, was found guilty in an English court of libelling Napoleon – but he was not punished, as Britain and France were at war at the time.

The ancestral home of the Washington family, of which the first president of the United States was a member, is in Sulgrave, Northamptonshire. They were aristocrats who emigrated to America after the execution of King Charles I.

In the Philippines, people can vote in elections at the age of only 15.

► Until his death in 1987, the only prisoner in Spandau prison in Berlin was the former Nazi Rudolf Hess. A prison staff of 105 were needed to keep him there. On Hess's death, the prison was pulled down.

A 19th-century Maharajah of Jaipur in India was so suspicious of foreign drinking water that whenever he went travelling he took with him several giant urns filled with water from the river Ganges.

▼ Sir Winston Churchill hated this portrait of him by Sir Walter Sickert. Another portrait Churchill disliked, by Graham Sutherland, was destroyed by Lady Churchill, despite being worth £150,000.

The smallest baby to have survived was born in England on 5th June 1938, weighing only 283 g (10 oz). The heaviest birth on record is that of a 10.7 kg (23¾ lb) baby born in the USA in 1879.

'Good King Wenceslas' was not a king at all but a prince of Bohemia who lived during the 10th century.

Since the Norman Conquest, five English kings have been deposed: Edward II in 1327, Richard III in 1399, Henry VI in 1460, Charles I in 1649, and James II in 1688.

When Captain James Cook first arrived in Hawaii, the natives believed him to be Lono, the god of fertility. When the Hawaiians realized their mistake, Cook was struck down and killed. Another explorer, the Spaniard Hernando Cortes, was mistaken by the Aztecs for the god Quetzalcoatl, who was said to be white and wear a beard. The Aztec emperor Montezuma greeted the Spaniards peacefully – enabling them to take him prisoner and conquer his lands.

About Places

A coal seam 152 m (500 ft) below the ground at Mount Wingen, Australia, has been burning for several thousand years. The site is called 'Burning Mountain'.

Alaska, the 49th state of the United States, was once Russian territory. It was bought from Russia in 1867 for $7,200,000 – a bargain, at less than $5 per square kilometre!

New York was first called New Amsterdam, because it was settled by the Dutch. When the settlement was taken over by the English, they named it after James, Duke of York.

After activity from Mount Pelée, the volcano near St Pierre, Martinique, more than 100 poisonous fer-de-lance snakes invaded the town, killing 50 residents. A month later the volcano erupted and all but two of the town's population lost their lives.

A milestone dating back to AD 150 is still in position near Bardon Mill, in the north of England.

The world's smallest independent country is the Vatican City State, in the centre of Rome. It is only 44 hectares (108 acres) in size.

The first English-speaking child born in America was called Virginia Dare, born on Roanoke Island on 18th August 1587. Soon afterwards, some of the settlers left for England to fetch supplies. When they returned two years later, Roanoke was deserted, and no trace of the settlers was ever found.

An English lord, Lord Baltimore, was granted a large area of land in Virginia, North America, by King Charles I. He wanted to call it 'Crescentia', but the king insisted that the area be named after his queen, Henrietta Maria – so it became known as 'Maryland' instead.

In 1893, an Australian named William Lane led a group of settlers to Paraguay, where they founded a colony they called New Australia, 135 km (84 miles) from Asunción.

There are statues on Easter Island, a tiny island in the Pacific, which weigh about 45 tonnes and stand 6m (20ft) high. Nobody knows who built them, or why, or why they abandoned their work before it was finished.

Somewhere beneath London there is a huge lake, thought by geologists to be part of a subterranean lake which stretches all the way beneath France.

▲ The station sign at the Welsh village of Llanfairpwllgwyngyllgogerychwyrndrobwll-llantysiliogogogoch – or 'Lllanfair PG', as it is known for short. The name means 'The Church of St Mary, in a hollow of white hazel, near to the rapid whirlpool and to St Tysilio Church, near to a red cave'.

◄ A view of the world's hottest place: Death Valley in the USA. Summer temperatures there reach 57°C (135°F), and the valley has only 5cm (2in) rainfall per annum.

The world's largest freshwater lake is Lake Superior, in North America, with an area of 82,103 sq km (31,700 sq miles). The lake is partly in Canada and partly in the United States and is 182m (597ft) above sea level.

The Egyptian obelisk in the Place de la Concorde, Paris, erected in 1833, is used as a giant sundial, the pavement around it being marked with the hours of the day.

'Dresden china' is not made at Dresden – but at Meissen, 20 km (13 miles) away.

▲ The action of the waves on the soft rock of the island of Heligoland in the North Sea has dramatically reduced its circumference, from about 190km (120 miles) in AD 800, to only 5km (3 miles) today.

About Buildings

The famous 'leaning tower' at Pisa in Italy was originally built as a bell tower, and was completed in the 14th century. It has slowly become more and more tilted, and is now about 5.6 m (18 ft) out of true.

Knole House, a stately home in England, has 365 rooms, 52 staircases, and 7 courtyards – one for each day of the year, one for each week of the year, and one for each day of the week!

At nearly 170 km (105 miles), the West Delaware water supply tunnel in New York City is the world's longest tunnel. The longest conventional railway tunnel is the Seikan Rail Tunnel, running beneath the Tsugaru Strait in Japan, at 58.9 km (33.5 miles). The longest road tunnel is the St Gotthard tunnel in Switzerland, which runs for 16 km (10 miles) and cost £176,600,000 to build. In 1985 plans were announced for the 50 km (30 mile) Eurotunnel, to run under the English Channel, between Britain and France.

▲ In 1975, the whole of a 400-year old church in Czechoslovakia was moved 730 m (800 yards) to a new site.

The clock tower at the Houses of Parliament in London is referred to as 'Big Ben'. 'Big Ben' is in fact the name of the bell inside, and is named after Sir Benjamin Hall, a tall and rather fat man who was commissioner of works when the bell was cast.

The lighthouse at the island of Pharos was one of the seven wonders of the ancient world. It was built of white marble, and stood 134 m (440 ft) high. Fires were lit at the top to guide seamen.

There are two obelisks called Cleopatra's Needle, one standing in London and one in New York. Neither has anything at all to do with Cleopatra, but were dedicated to the pharaoh Thothmes III.

The Great Wall of China is 2400 km (1500 miles) or more in length, 12 m (40 ft) high, and 4.5 m (15 ft) across – remarkable for a structure built in the third century BC.

Another remarkable ancient structure is the great pyramid at Giza, Egypt, which is 230 m (750 ft) square, and made of about 2,300,000 blocks of stone, each weighing $2\frac{1}{4}$ tonnes.

and Other Structures

◀ The oldest and the longest: Ironbridge, over the river Severn at Coalbrookdale in England, was the first major bridge to be built of iron, in 1779. The Humber suspension bridge, over the Humber estuary on Britain's east coast (below) has the longest single span in the world, of 1410m (4626ft). It was opened in 1981.

▼ The Pineapple, a two-storey summer house at Dunmore in Scotland, was so carefully built that every leaf is separately drained to prevent damage by accumulated water or frost. It was built in 1761.

The world's largest cathedral is St John the Divine in New York. Work on the building started in 1892 and took so long that people referred to the cathedral as 'St John the Unfinished'. Its nave is the world's longest, measuring 183m (600ft).

Saint Sophia at Istanbul was built in AD 532–537 as a Christian cathedral. It has since been a Islamic mosque, and is now a museum.

▼ Britain's tallest toy! This tower at Waterloo station is built entirely of Lego bricks and is 15.1 m (50 ft) high. There's an even taller one in Tel Aviv, measuring 18.15 m (59.5 ft) in height.

The Colossus of Rhodes was a huge statue of the sun god Helios, 52 m (170 ft) high. It took 12 years to build, and was completed in the year 304 BC. It was destroyed by an earthquake some 500 years later.

The interior of the Vertical Assembly Building, constructed to hold four of the giant Saturn V rockets built by Nasa to send men to the moon, is so vast that a special air-conditioning system had to be designed to stop clouds forming and rain falling – inside the building!

The world's largest theatre is in Perth, Western Australia, and can seat over 8000 people in front of a stage covering 1150 sq m (12,000 sq ft). The oldest indoor theatre in the world is the Teatro Olimpico at Vicenza in Italy, built in 1583.

In High Places

The tallest tower of any kind in the world is a radio mast 96 km (60 miles) from Warsaw, in Poland. It stands 646 m (2120 ft) high and is supported by 15 guy ropes. The tallest free-standing building is the 555 m (1822 ft) CN Tower in Toronto, Canada (see right). It includes a viewing platform 347 m (1140 ft) from the ground. The record for an occupied building is held by the Sears Tower, in Chicago in the USA, which stands 443 m (1454 ft) high, and has 110 storeys. It was completed in 1973. The twin towers of the World Trade Centre in New York City are nearly as tall, at 411 m (1350 ft). The World Trade Centre complex houses 35,000 workers, and receives an additional 80,000 visitors every day.

The history of building high is closely associated with the limited space of New York's Manhattan Island. Until 1929, the highest structure was the Eiffel Tower in Paris, at 300 m (985 ft). Then the Chrysler Building, at 318 m (1046 ft), and the Empire State Building at 381 m, (1250 ft) were built, giving New York the beginning of its unique skyline. Recently, a giant inflatable model of 'King Kong', the monster featured in the film of the same name, was attached to the outside of the Empire State Building, imitating a famous scene from the film. The stunt ran into problems, however, because it was difficult to keep the giant balloon inflated and in position.

◀ The 555m (1822ft) CN Tower on the edge of Lake Ontario in Toronto, Canada, cost about $44 million and was finished in 1975. It is a broadcasting station for television signals.

▲ The Tibi Dam, near Alicante in Spain, was built in 1594, and has worked succesfully ever since. This prototype for modern dam-builders is 33m (111ft) thick at the base.

The tallest cathedral spire in the world is that of Ulm cathedral in Germany, which stretches to 160m (528ft).

In 1945 a B-52 bomber hit the Empire State Building in New York, then the tallest building in the world, killing 14 people.

The first London Bridge was almost certainly constructed of wood, and was built between AD 100 and 400 during the Roman occupation. It was burnt down several centuries later, in 1014.

About the World and the Universe

Light travels 299,728 km (186,282 miles) *every second* – about 26 million km in a day, or nearly 10 billion km in a year. Astronomers measure *distances* in 'light years' – meaning the distance travelled by light in a year. The nearest star to the Earth, apart from the Sun, is about four light years away. Because it has taken four years for the light from the star to reach the Earth, we see it as it was four years ago, and we see very distant objects in the night sky, such as the famous Andromeda Galaxy, as they were thousands of years ago. Even light from the sun takes eight minutes to reach the Earth.

Energy

A person walking into a crowded room produces extra heat equivalent to turning on two 60-watt light bulbs.

At the estuary of the river Rance in France, a power station converts the rise and fall of the tides into electrical energy.

In the United States, experiments are being carried out with huge floating power stations which turn the heat of warm areas of the sea, such as the Gulf Stream, into electricity.

In only two or three days, the Earth receives energy from the Sun equal to that which would be produced by burning all the wood, coal and oil it possesses.

◀ **This 18 m (61 ft) high 'egg-beater' windmill produces 60 watts of electricity.**

The planet Jupiter is some 300 times the size of the Earth. In 1944, scientists discovered that the star known as 61 Cygni B is orbited by a planet 15 times the size of Jupiter.

Water is everywhere! It covers two-thirds of the Earth's surface and makes up 70% of the human body. In fact, water is probably the most common chemical compound in the Universe because the two substances from which it is made are themselves the most common (hydrogen) and the third-most common (oxygen) elements.

◀ There are deep underground streams beneath some parts of the dry Sahara Desert. People digging for fresh water have actually caught live fish!

The Amazon river is so powerful that *fresh* water can be taken from the sea and drunk 160km (100 miles) from the river mouth.

If *all* the substances produced when an object is burned are carefully collected together and weighed, it will be found that the object is heavier than it was before it was set alight. This is because oxygen combines with things when they are burned.

The Soviet space station Mir was launched in 1986. Since then, two space endurance records have been set. In 1987, Leonid Kizim spent $326\frac{1}{2}$ days there, and in 1989 two Soviet astronauts stayed there for a total of 366 days.

It has been estimated that the number of living things occupying the Earth, not including human beings, is in the region of 3,000,000,000,000,000,000,000,000,000,000, – or 3000 quintillion.

In Iceland, there are places where hot springs rise through the Earth's crust beneath glaciers – so it is possible to take a hot bath in a cave made of ice!

Amazing Voyage! The space probe Voyager 2 sent back this picture of the planet Saturn in August 1981. The craft was launched in 1977, flew past Jupiter in July 1979, then used the gravitational pull of Saturn to send it on a new course towards the planet Uranus. In 1986, 9 years after its launch, the craft sent back detailed pictures of Uranus and its moons, before heading towards Neptune, which it passed in 1989. The flight path has been astonishingly accurate: Uranus is only a small planet at 50,000km (32,000 miles) across, and it is over a billion kilometres from the Earth – yet Voyager passed within 80,000km (50,000 miles) of the planet's surface.

Radio waves travel at the speed of light, but sound only travels at about 1100km/h (700mph). This means that a live radio show broadcast in London *could* be heard by listeners in New York before it is heard on the other side of the room in which it is taking place.

When the radiation in stars starts to die down, they collapse in a massive explosion called a 'supernova'. All that is left is a small but incredibly dense globe known as a neutron star. A piece of neutron star the size of a pinhead would weigh as much as a supertanker. Gravity there is so strong that the forces which created Mount Everest on Earth would raise a lump only two centimetres high – and it would take a human more than a lifetime's energy to climb it.

About Animals

A crocodile's jaws are strong enough to break a person's leg – but only when *closing*. The muscles which open a crocodile's mouth are quite weak, and the animal's mouth could be held closed with one hand.

A tortoise which died in Devon, England in 1977 had lived for over 116 years.

It has been estimated that there are an average of 50,000 spiders per acre of green land, and that they destroy 100 times their number in insects.

The dromedary is a one-humped Arabian camel which is specially bred for speed. A good one can run 110 km (70 miles) a day.

The water flea of northern Europe measures a mere 0.25 mm (0.1 in) from top to toe. This means it would take nearly 16,000 water fleas standing on each others backs to reach the shoulder of the tallest elephant ever seen, a 4 m (13 ft) giant shot in Angola in 1974.

A mollusc called the sea hare can lay over a million eggs a day.

The coelacanth is a fish which was believed to have been extinct for 60 million years – but it had been regularly caught by fishermen off the coast of South Africa, a fact not discovered by scientists until 1938.

The world's oldest cat was owned by a lady from Devon, England, whose pet died in 1939 at the age of 36 years.

An elephant's trunk has 40,000 muscles.

► The okapi, which lives in the rain forests of Zaire, looks a little like a zebra but is in fact the only relative of the giraffe. The giraffe itself has a very big heart which is needed to pump blood up its long neck to its head. On average, a giraffe's heart is 60cm (2ft) long and has walls 7.5cm (3in) thick.

◄ The largest blue whale ever seen was over 33m (110ft) long. These whales are the largest of all animals.

◄ Sea anemones are animals, not plants. They feed by catching small creatures in their tentacles. They are poisonous, and their touch can cause a severe rash.

fobhríste

The most venomous snake is Belcher's sea snake. Its poison is 100 times more potent than that of the most dangerous land snake, the western taipan, found in Australia.

Water beetles can actually eat small fish and frogs. This mostly applies to large South American varieties, some of which are 100mm (4in) long, but even small water beetles will eat tiny fish and tadpoles.

The pig has been bred in captivity in China since about 4000 BC.

The owner of a white Samoyed dog, who lived at Felpham in England, was for years able to spin his dog's hair into thread and make it into socks, scarves, gloves and jumpers.

The turkey is a native of America. It was not brought to Europe until the beginning of the 16th century.

The world's longest earthworm is found in South Africa. One found in 1937 measured a staggering 6.7m (22ft) in length and 20mm (0.78in) in diameter.

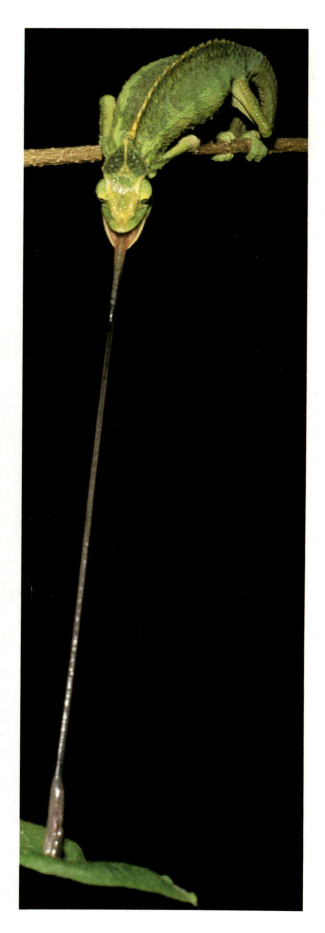

Most sea snakes give birth to live young. They have a body flattened from side to side, and can lie on the surface of the water, taking in air.

During the First World War, parrots were kept at the top of the Eiffel Tower in Paris. With their acute hearing, they could hear enemy aircraft long before human beings themselves could hear them and so warn of their approach.

Although large enough – up to 450 kg (1000 lb) in weight and 4 m (13 ft) in length – to be able to swallow a person whole, the giant grouper fish is fairly harmless. It is, however, quite fearless, and has a sinister reputation for stalking skin-divers.

As many as 40,000 people die from snake-bites every year.

The duck-billed platypus of Australia is one of nature's oddities, for it has a furry coat, a tail like a beaver, burrows in the ground but is equally at home in water. It lays eggs, but suckles its young like other mammals. Another unusual creature is the echidna, or spiny anteater, of Tasmania, which has sharp spines like a hedgehog, lays eggs and suckles its young. Like the platypus, it is a mammal, but has padded feet, strong claws and a sticky tongue for snatching up insects.

The hyrax is a tiny mammal living in Africa and Australia. It looks like a marmot, has a skeleton like a rhinoceros and is probably the only animal related to the e'

The bluefish western Atlantic Ocean is the out one billion – and each b eat ten other fish *every day.*

◀ The chameleon can change colour to suit its surroundings or its mood and can move one eye without moving the other. Its tongue shoots out at lightning speed to grab food, reaching a length longer than the animal itself!

Shark!

The dwarf shark is surprisingly small, growing to only 30 cm (1 ft) in length. The common dogfish is also a species of small shark.

The great white shark, made famous in the film Jaws, can reach 11 m (36 ft) in length, and will eat anything – including man.

Sharks have no bones, only a flexible skeleton made of cartilage. They also have very rough skin – like sandpaper.

Less than 10% of the world's sharks are actually dangerous to man. The most dangerous is the grey nurse shark.

The hammerhead shark's head has projections on each side, making it look like a hammer. Its eyes are on the end of these projections.

The largest shark is the whale shark, which reaches 18 m (60 ft) in length and $13\frac{1}{2}$ tonnes in weight. It feeds on plankton.

◄ This *is* a shark – a wobbegong shark. They are also called 'carpet sharks', because of their broad, fringed heads and their carpet-like appearance. The pattern is actually a camouflage that enables the wobbegong to sneak up on its prey.

In 1839, an American traveller recorded taking three days to pass through a single herd of buffalo. It has been estimated from his account that the herd contained a million or more animals and covered an area of as much as 3000 sq km (1300 sq miles).

► A female pigeon has to be able to see another pigeon before she can lay her eggs – although seeing her reflection in a mirror will work if there are no other pigeons around!

About Plants

The dwarf willow tree, which grows in mountain areas, reaches a height of only a few centimetres.

Bamboo grows very fast, sometimes as much as a metre in a day. Bamboo plants only flower at long intervals. Some varieties flower every 32 years; others only every 60 years.

Kapok is a fluffy material which comes from the silk cotton tree. It is totally immune to attack by insects and pests, and is used for stuffing furniture.

Woad is a strong dark blue dye, and was used by ancient Britons to stain their bodies. The staining is very powerful and will only disappear when new skin grows. Indigo, a dark blue dye, can be obtained from the woad plant. Queen Elizabeth I of England so disliked the disgusting smell produced when the plant is prepared that she banned woad-growing within five miles of all her residences.

Although the sequoia tree will grow for centuries, its wood is very brittle. If the tree falls over, it cracks into small pieces.

The leaves of the giant water lily plant grow to be as much as 2.5 m (8 ft) across.

Hops did not come into use for flavouring beer until the 16th century. Henry VIII actually forbade English brewers to use them.

Holly was once called the 'Holy Tree' because of a legend that it first sprang up in the footsteps of Jesus Christ. The prickly leaves and red berries were said to symbolize the crown of thorns and Christ's suffering.

The seeds of the lotus flower can 'live' for more than a hundred years.

The aristolochia is sometimes called the 'Dutchman's pipe' because of its shape. Its scent, which is like rotting meat, is very unpleasant to humans – but it attracts flies, which pollinate the flowers.

◄ In parts of tropical Africa there is a tree known as the sausage tree, on account of the shape of its fruit. The 'sausage' grows to about 76 cm (2½ ft) in length.

▶ The most massive living thing on the Earth is the 'General Sherman', a giant redwood tree in California 83m (272ft) high and 24m (78ft) round. It contains enough wood to make 500 million pencils, and has been alive for over 4000 years. This cross-section of the trunk shows some of the events that have taken place during the tree's life.

One type of South American nut is called the Monkey's Dinner Bell because it explodes with a loud bang, hurling its kernels in all directions.

The date palm thrives only in dry, desert areas. If rain falls when the fruit are ripe, the whole crop is ruined.

Dr Nemce, a Czech chemist, established that plants growing in gold-bearing soil do contain gold.

The peanut sets its own seeds by burying its pods in the ground.

▶ The tallest redwood tree in the world reached a height of over 112m (367ft) in 1963 before it started to die back.

▼ This fly is being eaten by a plant called a Venus Fly Trap. When a fly lands on the plant's tiny hairs, the plant closes and digests the unlucky insect. There are several species of carnivorous plants – even in Britain, where some marsh grasses feed on insects.

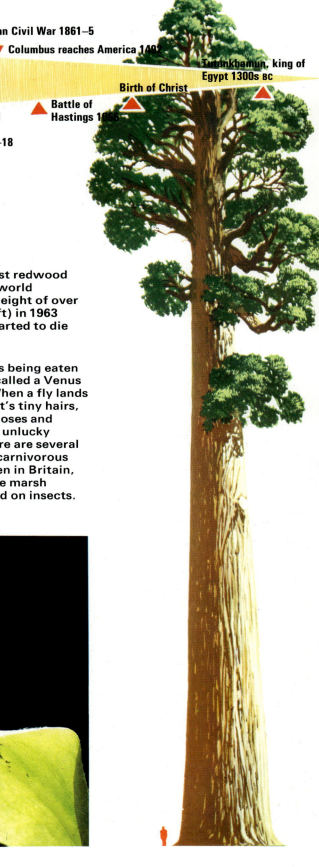

◀ The rafflesia plant has the biggest flowers in the world. They are 90cm (3ft) across and weigh as much as 7kg (15lb). They also have an appalling smell, and are sometimes called 'stinking corpse lilies'.

The oak tree was once highly valued for its acorns (a fine pig food) rather than for its timber.

The very earliest paper-like material was papyrus, made from the pith of the papyrus plant. It is a species of sedge, once common in the Nile delta region. Another source of writing material is esparto, a grass which grows in Mediterranean countries. Esparto is used for making high-quality printing paper.

The morning glory plant is so called because it lasts only a few hours.

Quinine comes from the bark of the cinchona tree, grown in the jungles of Peru. It was welcomed in the 19th century as a cure for malaria.

A plant belonging to the mimosa family is known as the 'sensitive plant' because if it is approached it will shrink away as if frightened. If touched, it shrivels up.

The poison used on arrows by tribes in East Africa came from an extract of the bark and seeds of the kombe tree. The poison, which can kill in minutes, is valued as a drug for use in the treatment of heart disease.

The segments of an orange were known as 'pigs' during the 19th century. The word has also been used to describe pieces of apple, a block of iron, certain kinds of earthenware pot, a bundle of hemp, a cube of salt – and an English sixpence!

The timber of the balsa tree is lighter than cork, which is the bark of the cork-oak tree. Balsa grows in the tropics at the astonishing speed of 4.5m (15ft) per year.

Mandrake, a plant of the potato family, has roots which look vaguely like the human form. Superstitious people once thought that the root would shriek if it was pulled out of the ground.

Rubber is the milky juice of a plant native to South America, which when dried becomes elastic. At one time, rubber could only be obtained from South America, but the seeds were secretly taken to London and then Malaysia, where the rubber industry is now very large.

The World in Danger

There are between five and ten million different species of living things on the Earth. This includes perhaps 350,000 plants and 45,000 different vertebrate animals; the rest are invertebrate animals such as insects. Some scientists have estimated that the rate at which species become extinct as their habitats are destroyed may have reached one every day.

Every year the nations of the world spend about £5 billion on weapons – that's about £100 for every man, woman and child.

Almost half the people of the world lack clean water to drink and proper sanitation. Just 30 weeks spending on weapons would provide these facilities, so that everybody could have clean water; three weeks arms spending would fund the United Nations' water supply projects for ten years.

'Acid rain' is produced where industries burn large amounts of coal, polluting the atmosphere with sulphur gas. In turn, the rain pollutes lakes and rivers. In Sweden, as many as 18,000 lakes have been seriously damaged in this way.

The world's cars pump about 250,000 tonnes of lead into the atmosphere every year. Lead has always been added to petrol to improve it, but scientists have now developed types of 'unleaded' petrol.

▼ **Every minute, about 40 hectares (100 acres) of the world's tropical rain forest is destroyed. At this rate, it is possible that all the rain forests in the world will have been destroyed by the year 2025. About half the world's species of animals and plants depend upon these forests for their survival. This picture shows a road cutting its way into the Amazon rain forest in South America.**

About Food and Drink

The puffer, or blowfish, is one of the world's most poisonous fish – yet it is regularly eaten in Japan, where it is regarded as a great delicacy. Known as *fugu*, the dish must be prepared by an expert chef, who removes the poison. Even so, people die from blowfish poisoning every year. The Greenland shark is also poisonous, but it too is often eaten, by Eskimos and other Arctic-dwellers. It must be cooked for several hours before it is eaten.

When the emperor Charles V of Spain was first offered a pineapple, he suspected somebody was trying to poison him and so he refused it.

Ice cream, blancmange, table jelly and other sweets are often made from 'Irish moss' – a type of seaweed, also called carrageen.

▼ Ships biscuits lasted almost forever – but were almost impossible to eat!

Shredded Wheat, the world's first ready-to-eat breakfast cereal, was invented by a man called H. D. Perky in Denver, Colorado, in 1893. Another famous American product, Coca Cola, was invented in 1886. It was marketed as an 'Esteemed Brain Tonic and Intellectual Beverage'!

The durian, a fruit from Malaysia, has a disgusting taste and smell. Yet there are people who have acquired a taste for it and consider it the most delicious of fruits.

Grapefruit once had the rather lengthy name of 'The Forbidden Fruit of Barbados'. The word 'grapefruit' was first used in 1814.

The blue veins and patches in many cheeses are caused by a mould, related to the drug penicillin.

The prickly pear is sometimes called the tuna fig – but it is not a pear, nor is it related to the fig plant. It is the fruit of the cactus and tastes like cucumber.

▶ *Vermicelli* is the Italian name for a very thin kind of spaghetti; it means 'little worms'. Spaghetti is thought of as Italian – but in fact pasta is eaten all over the world, and comes in many shapes, colours, sizes – and even flavours! There is one type made from chocolate paste.

While out in the wilds and short of food Bishop Stringer of the Yukon had to stew his spare pair of boots and eat them!

The world's heaviest coffee drinkers are the Finns, who consume an average of 37g (1.3oz) per person per day. The world's heaviest drinkers of beer are the Bavarians, from Southern Germany.

The roots of the dandelion can be roasted and used to make dandelion coffee, which some people cannot distinguish from the real thing. In fact, many people prefer it because it contains no caffeine.

Popcorn is not a modern invention. It is made from the grains of maize, and has been eaten in South America since the days of the great Inca empire.

Bombay duck comes from Bombay – but it is not duck. It's dried fish!

The grape was certainly one of the first fruits to be used for making wine and remains by far the best. Both the ancient Greeks and the ancient Romans perfected the craft of wine making. Roman wines were highly prized, both for their flavour and their long life. Stored in tightly sealed earthenware jars some varieties would keep and improve for 100 years or more.

Spices, such as cinnamon, cloves, nutmeg and pepper, were once bought from Arab traders. They were expensive, which was one reason why people considered it worthwhile making the voyages of discovery which found their origin.

In Arabia, locusts are captured, their wings and legs removed, and the bodies fried in butter and eaten.

Hungry?

A publicity stunt at a supermarket in Belgium in 1984 involved the cooking of a giant 35,000 – egg omelette! In America recently, egg manufacturers have been trying to persuade people to buy eggs ready-whipped, in cartons rather like those used to sell milk. In France, it has been possible to buy omelettes in a *tube* since 1980. Other foods available in tubes include honey, onion paste, garlic paste and tomato paste.

About Inventions and Discoveries

The world's first submarine was built as long ago as 1624, by a Dutchman called Cornelius Drebbel. It was operated by 12 men rowing through sealed portholes.

... And the world's first vacuum cleaner was invented and put on sale in 1902 by Henry Booth, a Londoner whose usual profession was designing bridges.

◀ The world's biggest barrel? This structure floats in the North Sea, in the Brent oil field, and is used to store oil before it is transfered to the shore by ship. It weighs 66,000 tonnes.

When bathtubs were first installed in the United States in the early part of the 19th century, newspapers attacked the idea as being 'undemocratic'. In 1843, the state of Virginia taxed the owners of bathtubs $30 per year for the privilege!

A ship's 'log', the instrument which measures the vessel's speed and the distance it has travelled, was originally a log-like piece of wood, attached to a cord with knots tied in it at intervals, and thrown into the sea. The number of knots paid out over a fixed period of time enabled the crew to work out the ship's speed – hence the term 'knot', meaning one nautical mile per hour.

When Henry Ford started his automobile factory in 1903, he had only 12 employees. Soichiro Honda, founder of the giant Japanese motorcycle firm, also began with only a dozen workers and a batch of second-hand engines which he fitted to lightweight frames.

▼ The world's longest car is the 16m (55ft) long 'Ultra Limo', built in California. It has an oven, a sink, a refrigerator, four telephones – and a 3.6m (12ft) swimming pool!

The supersonic airliner *Concorde* actually gets several centimetres longer when it is flying at full speed. This is because the friction between the plane and the atmosphere causes the metal to heat up and expand.

Leonardo da Vinci was not only a painter. He designed a variety of objects, including machine guns, helicopters, parachutes and paddle-wheel boats. Few of these machines were ever tried. Leonardo's imagination ran far ahead of the technical possibilities of his time.

The pillar-box, as used by the British post-office, was invented by a novelist, Anthony Trollope, who was also a postal official.

The ballot-box, now used for voting throughout the world, was invented in Victoria, Australia, in 1856.

▼ The eccentric and reclusive millionaire Howard Hughes designed and had built this giant seaplane, intending to use it as a troop carrier. It had a wing span of nearly 100m (328ft) and eight engines. It was called the 'Spruce Goose', and flew once, when Hughes himself was the pilot, for a distance of about 1.6km (1 mile). The plane has remained in storage ever since.

Postal services existed as early as the year 500 BC in ancient Persia, where runners carried messages for the king and the government's officials. The Greek historian Herodotus wrote: 'neither snow nor rain nor heat nor gloom of night stays these couriers from the swift completion of their appointed rounds'. These words can be seen today – carved above the entrance to the General Post Office in New York City.

▲ The world's first photograph took over eight hours to expose! It was taken by a Frenchman, Joseph Nicephore Niepce, and showed the courtyard of a country house – so nobody actually had to stand still for that long.

The country with the most television sets in the world is the tiny Pacific island of Guam, where there are 700 sets for every 1000 people. Monaco, on the edge of the Mediterranean, is the only country with *more* telephones than people – there are 1071 for every 1000 of the population.

Getting About

◀ Sail rail! Early travellers on the Kansas-Pacific railroad in the United States used the wind to propel them.

The world's first motorcycle was made of wood. It was built by the German, Gottlieb Daimler, in 1885, and was used to test his new four-stroke petrol engine.

The great iron sailing ships known as 'windjammers' had over 60 tonnes of rigging and carried over an acre (0.4 hectares) of sail. Despite having all this gear to manage, they often had only small crews. There is a record of one sailing round Cape Horn with only 19 men aboard.

The forerunner of the modern bicycle was the velocipede, demonstrated in Paris in 1791, which looked like a bike, but was propelled by the rider's feet running along the ground. It was not until 1839, when Kirkpatrick MacMillan added some pedals, that the modern bicycle was invented.

At Wuppertal in Germany, the river valley is too narrow for an underground railway, so a monorail system has been built running above the streets and waterways, instead of below.

In 1919, an Italian engineer called Caproni built a giant 9-wing, 100-seater, seaplane. Unfortunately, it was too heavy to fly.

▶ Crossing the Irish Sea – by Volkswagen!

▲ This is the world's most economical petrol-engined vehicle. Its capacity is only 15 cc, and in 1984 it completed 3803 miles on a single gallon of fuel at the Silverstone racing circuit in England, travelling at between 21 and 35 km/h (13–22 mph).

The world's first general purpose electronic computer, called EINAC, contained 19,000 valves, producing as much heat as 150 electric fires. The first commercially available computer was built in 1950 and cost around £1,000,000; today, only 40 years later, a similarly powerful table-top model can be bought in the shops for about £100.

The first commercial ship to use sails as a means of propulsion to be launched for more than 50 years began sea-trials in 1980. The 1600-ton Japanese tanker *Shin-Aitoku Maru* uses huge rigid sails, controlled by electric motors linked to a computer, as well as ordinary engines, to save fuel. It has been estimated that if all the commercial shipping in the world were powered in this way, as much as 150 million tonnes of oil might be saved every year.

One of the first showers was installed at Chatsworth, the home of the English aristocrat the Duke of Devonshire. The device required somebody to pump it by hand. Steam baths became popular in the 1890s, in a design that could only be opened from the outside. This meant that there was no escape for the bather if the fire providing the steam got out of control!

A giant 'Jumbo Tron' television was constructed by the Japanese firm Sony in 1985, measuring 42 m (138 ft) in height and with an area of over 1000 sq m (10,000 sq ft). The smallest colour television produced to date has a screen 38 mm (1.5 in) across.

The 18th-century English astronomer Sir Edmund Halley, who gave his name to Halley's Comet, invented the diving bell. It was a large wooden barrel filled with air and weighted so it would sink. Extra air was supplied from barrels sunk to a lower level than the main bell and attached to it by a pipe. Divers could leave the chambers and walk on the river bottom while breathing air through a tube.

About Entertainment

The world's first television advertiser was a maker of permanent waves for hairdressing, who had the idea for a hairdressing fair at London's Olympia in 1930.

The Archers, a British radio show first broadcast in 1950, is the longest-running radio show, having been transmitted over 36,000 times. Only one actor, Norman Painting, who plays Philip Archer, has survived from the first episode.

The longest running television show is the American programme *Meet the Press*, which has been transmitted weekly since 1948.

The Mousetrap, a play by the late Agatha Christie, has been running in London for about 40 years, completing in the region of 19,000 performances since it opened in 1952.

In 1960, Bing Crosby, the American singer, received a platinum disc to commemorate the sale of his 200,000,000th record.

▲ The character of Sherlock Holmes has appeared in over 170 films, and been played by more than 60 actors.

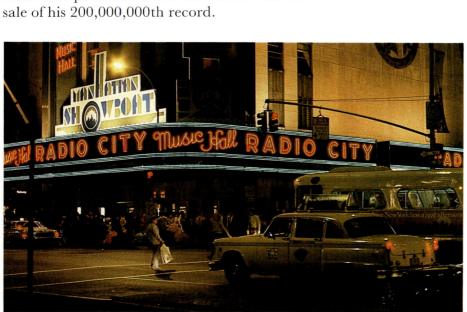

◀ The world's biggest cinema, the famous Radio City Music Hall on Broadway in New York City, can seat 5800 people.

The composer Wolfgang Amadeus Mozart was playing the harpsichord by ear at the age of three, and enough of his early compositions have survived to show that he had a thorough grasp of music by the age of five. It is less well-known that Mozart had a talented sister, Maria Anna, born in 1751, who, like her brother, could play and compose at a remarkably early age.

Silent film star Rudolf Valentino's real name was Rudolpho Alfonso Raffaelo Pierre Filbert Guglielmo di Valentina d'Antonguolla.

The first woman known to have written a play and had it performed was Mrs Aphra Behn, whose *The Forced Marriage; or, The Jealous Bridegroom* ran for six days at the Duke's Theatre, London, in 1670.

The international language Esperanto has sometimes been used in films when an unrecognisable 'foreign'-sounding language has been required. These include *Idiot's Delight* (1939), *State Secret* (1950), *Incubus* (1965) and *The Great Dictator* (1940), in which it appeared on the shop signs.

Theodore Roosevelt was the first American president to become an actor, when he played himself in a short comedy made in 1908. Ronald Reagan is the first actor to have become the US president!

Aïda, the opera by the Italian composer Giuseppe Verdi, was specially written for the opening of the Suez Canal in 1871. The opera is set in ancient Egypt, and was first performed at the Cairo Opera House.

When a play called *Bag* opened at a theatre in Grantham, England, not a single member of the public turned up to see it.

The 'Piccolo' ('small') Theatre in Hamburg has room for only 30 people in the auditorium.

Film Facts

In the film The Gold Rush, *made in 1924, Charlie Chaplin eats his boots. They were made of liquorice.*

Edgar Wallace has had over 150 of his plays, stories and novels made into films.

Only six of Shakespeare's plays have not *been filmed.*

The character of Napoleon has appeared in more than 160 films, Hitler and Lenin in 55 films each, Queen Victoria of England in 36 films, and the American president Abraham Lincoln in 128 films.

Rescued by Rover, a British film made in 1905, cost only seven pounds, thirteen shillings, and nine pence. The most expensive film so far recorded is Rambo III, *which cost $69 million (£42 million) to make in 1988.*

The film Sebastiane, *made in Britain in 1976, was recorded entirely in Latin.*

In 1933, the cartoon character Mickey Mouse received more than 80,000 letters from adoring fans!

About Language and Literature

In the 1930s, a Belgian, Auguste Meunier, wrote 17,131 words on the back of an ordinary postcard. This achievement is, however, exceeded by that of Frank Watts of Norfolk, England, who managed to write the Lord's Prayer 34 times (nearly 9500 letters) in the area of a British Postage stamp – without glasses or any other aid.

Luck, rather than great commercial success kept the famous French impressionist painter Claude Monet financially secure: in 1891 he won 100,000 francs in a lottery, enabling him to spend his time painting, instead of worrying about paying the bills.

Bram Stoker, the author of *Dracula*, was unable to walk or stand until he was 17 years old – then he became a capable athlete and footballer!

An American novelist, Ernest Vincent Wright, wrote a novel in 1939 called *Gadsby*, in which the letter 'e' was totally omitted.

The world's greatest linguist was apparently Cardinal Giuseppe Gaspardo Mezzofanti (1744-1849), who mastered 58 languages, and was familiar with a total of 114 languages and dialects.

A painting by the French artist Henri Matisse, called *Le Bateau* (*The Boat*), was hung upside-down in the Museum of Modern Art in New York in 1961. It was 47 days before anyone noticed!

Ludovic Zamenhof, inventor of the international language Esperanto, completed his work as a young man. His father immediately threw the manuscript into the fire. Undeterred, Zamenhof began again, and eventually completed a new version.

It is said that a 10th-century ruler of Persia was so scholarly that he took his library with him on his travels – alphabetically arranged on a train of camels!

Unknown Women?

Jane Austen (below left) had four novels published during her lifetime – all without her name being mentioned. In the 19th century, writing was not considered a woman's profession, and several famous women writers used men's names. Emily Brontë, author of Wuthering Heights, *called herself 'Ellis Bell', and her sister Charlotte (centre left), who wrote* Jane Eyre, *took the name 'Currer Bell'. 'George Eliot' (centre right) was really Mary Ann Evans, and the French novelist 'George Sand' (right) was really Amandine Lucile Aurore.*

According to legend, the ancient Greek playwright Aeschylus was killed when an eagle mistook his bald head for a rock, and dropped a tortoise on it – presumably in an attempt to break the animal's shell open.

The shortest sentence in English containing all the 26 letters of the alphabet is 'Pack my box with five dozen liquor jugs'.

Vincent van Gogh, one of the 20th century's best-known painters, is believed to have sold only one picture during his lifetime.

Little Lord Fauntleroy, in the book of the same name, was modelled on the author's young son. He was Vivian Burnett, who grew up to become a famous athlete, and died in 1961, aged 61.

There is no word in the English language rhyming with 'orange'.

▼ **Pablo Picasso's painting** *The Studio*. **Picasso is reputed to have been the most productive artist of all time, creating as many as 13,000 paintings, 100,000 prints, 34,000 book illustrations and 300 sculptures in his lifetime.**

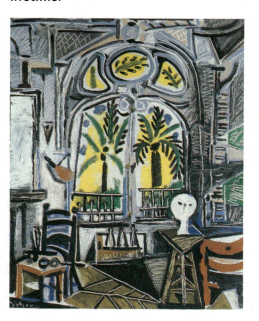

About Sport

The ball game called 'pelota', popular in parts of Spain, has a long history. It was invented in Italy, and played in France as early as the 13th century. A French king, Louis X, collapsed and died after playing *longue-paume*, a tennis-like version of pelota, in 1316. The modern game is said to be the world's fastest ball game, the ball reaching speeds as high as 300km/h (190mph).

During the reign of Edward III of England, the following games were banned, because of their association with gambling: football, stone-throwing, wood-throwing and iron-throwing, cambucam (a kind of golf), quoits, handball and club-ball.

Lacrosse was first played by the North American Indians, who gave the game the name *baggataway*.

At Isfahan in Iran, there are the remains of an ancient polo ground dating from over 2000 years ago.

Boris Becker, the German who became both the youngest-ever and the first unseeded tennis player to win the Wimbledon men's singles tennis competition in 1985, was several months younger than the *junior* champion at Wimbledon that year!

William Herbert Grace, doctor and cricketer, made 54,904 runs (including 126 centuries), took 2,876 wickets, and made 877 catches in his career. But perhaps the most remarkable cricketing record is Sir Donald Bradman's average test-match score of 99.94. Except for an uncharacteristically low score in his final innings, his average would have exceeded 100.

▼ **Seven men on a single pair of skis – but no snow in sight!**

In 1972 in Utah, the United States, a man called Allan Abbott managed to reach 222km/h (139mph) on a specially-designed pedal cycle.

In 1950, just under 200,000 people saw the soccer match played between Brazil and Uruguay at the Marcana Stadium in Rio de Janeiro, Brazil. The biggest sports crowd is probably the ten million or so people who turn out to see various stages of the *Tour de France* cycle race every summer.

In 1922, a British firm invented a golf ball equipped with a tiny parachute – a device which slowed the ball down and enabled beginners to practise at home without endangering their neighbours.

At about 5 hectares (12.4 acres) in area, a polo field is the largest pitch in sport.

In Sweden, in 1984, about 1700 competitors took part in a downhill skiing event!

▶ *Australia*, the predecessor of the 12-metre class yacht *Australia II* which ended the longest unbeaten record in sporting history when, after 132 years, it wrestled the America's Cup from the New York Yacht Club's *America*. 12-metre yachting is the world's most expensive sport. It costs many millions of pounds to design and race one of these boats.

The 'Red Hose' foot race has been held at Carnwath, Strathclyde, Scotland, every year since 1508.

Real tennis was once a very popular game, particularly in France. At the end of the 16th century, there were over 1800 courts in Paris alone. Today real tennis courts are less common. There are only three in England.

Golf is a very old game. It certainly existed under that name in 1457, when it was banned in Scotland by King James II.

▼ The University Boat Race between Oxford and Cambridge has been rowed since 1829. This picture shows the result of the most spectacular mistake in the race's history, when the Cambridge crew rowed into a large barge before the start of the 1984 race.

Passing the Time

Wasting Time?

A Greek monk, Simeon the Younger, is reported to have spent the last 45 years of his life on top of a pillar in Syria. He was nicknamed 'Stylites', from the Greek word *stylos*, meaning 'pillar'.

Tired of jogging? Why not get some 'Kangaroo Shoes'? These are boots with large curved 'springs' on the bottom. Instead of running, the wearer bounces along! The Canadian inventor claims this is excellent training for skiing, tennis, basketball and other sports.

Sea bathing only became popular as a recreation in the 19th century, when the invention of the railway enabled people to travel to the coast.

During the festival of St Firminus in the Spanish city of Pamplona, young bulls are released into the streets. Young men run ahead of the animals for as long as they dare, in what is considered a demonstration of fearlessness.

Lawn mower racing is becoming a popular sport in England. In the 1980 12-hour race at Wisborough Green in Sussex, a world-record distance of 444 km (276 miles) was achieved. Tractor pulling is another odd sport: huge, customized machines compete to see which can pull the greatest load. The biggest of these giants produce about 8000 horsepower!

In a number of places around the world, people like to swim outside all the year round. In Moscow, where winter temperatures can fall to −40°C, this means breaking through several inches of ice covering the lakes.

A man from Kent, England, spent two years, between 1982 and 1984, writing a letter to his wife, which eventually reached nearly one and a half million words in length.

▲ One of the most remarkable world records is Bob Beamon's massive 8.9-m (29 ft 2½ in) long jump, which has remained intact since it was set at the 1968 Olympic Games in Mexico City.

Remarkable Records

Paul Elvstrom of Denmark won four successive gold medals in the Olympic yachting event between 1948 and 1960. In 1984, he was still competing in the Olympics, sailing with his daughter as crew.

The world champion at real tennis, Frenchman Jacques Edmond Barre, held the championship for an amazing 33 years.

The highest score in a full international soccer match is England's 17–0 defeat of Australia in 1951.

The world's heaviest sportsman was the professional wrestler William J. Cobb of the USA, who weighed 363 kg (802 lb).

The highest test-match cricket score is one of 903, made by England against Australia in 1938.

The first gymnast to record the 'perfect' score of 10.0 was Nadia Comaneci, at the 1976 Montreal Olympic Games.

In 1840 two Nottingham men, called Bendigo and Caunt, staged a prizefight which eventually lasted 92 rounds and took over two hours to complete. Bendigo won, gaining the £400 prize money, together with a belt, and had a town in Australia named after him.

The first Derby race for horses was run in 1780, and was named after its founder, the Earl of Derby.

The highest recorded individual score in a cricket match is the 628 not out (out of a total of 836) in a match at a Bristol school in 1899. The scorer gave Arthur Collins' score as '628 – plus or minus 20'.

The highest speed reached by a human being is the 300 km/h (185 mph) achieved by skydivers. Skiers have been recorded at speeds well over 160 km/h (100 mph) – the fastest being the 223 km/h (139 mph) by Michael Prufer in 1988. Speed skaters have reached speeds of almost 50 km/h (30 mph), and the world 100 metre sprint record represents an average speed of about 36 km/h (22 mph).

The first man to swim across the English Channel was Captain Matthew Webb who, in 1875, made the crossing in 22 hours, despite being stung by fish on the way.

Badminton was given its name by the place in which the modern game started – Badminton Hall in Avon, the seat of the Duke of Beaufort, although a similar game was played in China as long ago as 2000 BC.

...And About Things

In 17th-century Russia, smoking was punishable by death after the third offence. In Turkey, offenders were hanged with a pipe thrust through their noses.

In the United States, 350 $10,000 bills remain in circulation, although no new ones have been issued since 1969. In 1776, a bank in Philadelphia issued bills in the rather odd denomination of six Spanish dollars. The USA did not issue its own banknotes until 1792.

In 1874, a group of eight pearls joined together in the shape of a cross was found inside an oyster at Raeburn, Western Australia. The pearls became famous, and were given the name 'The Southern Cross'.

In India, large numbers are calculated in 'crores' and 'lakhs', not hundreds, thousands and millions. A lakh is 100,000 and a crore 100 lakhs (or 10 million) – but the word lakh can also be used to describe any very large number.

Although the fighting stopped in 1918, the First World War was officially continued between Britain and Turkey until 1924, when the two countries finally signed a peace treaty.

The Russian national airline, Aeroflot, is the world's largest. It flies 1650 aircraft over a million kilometres (620,000 miles) every year, carrying about 119 million passengers and employing about 500,000 staff.

▼ **This is the only cable car in the world where passengers can take a bath! It crosses the Bay of Arita, near Osaka, in Japan.**

the World Over!

▶ The Medhane Alem ('Saviour of the world') church in Ethiopia is carved out of solid rock. It measures 33m (108ft) in length and 11m (36ft) in height, and its roof is level with the surrounding land. It is among Africa's oldest Christian churches.

◀ The Nullarbor Plain lies in Southern Australia. Its name comes from the Latin words *nulla arbor*, meaning 'no tree'. The trans-Australia railway, which crosses the plain, contains the world's longest stretch of straight track – 478km (298 miles) without a curve.

The Sphinx, a giant statue with the body of a lion and the face of a man which stands at Giza in Egypt, is about 4000 years old. The great riddle of the Sphinx is: What speaks with one voice, yet goes on four legs, then two, then three? Oedipus, the hero of a famous ancient Greek tragedy, gave the answer: Man. For he crawls on four legs as a child, goes upright on two legs as an adult, and walks on three (his own, plus a walking stick) when old.

In Riverside County, California, a stone monument stands in memory of the first orange tree to be imported into the USA from Brazil.

The Chinese have bred Pekinese dogs for over 5000 years.

The Cornish language became extinct when the last native speaker, Doll Pentreath, died in 1777 at the age of 91.

La Paz in Bolivia, at nearly 3700m (12,000ft) above sea level, is the world's highest capital city. The risk of a serious fire breaking out there is less than in other large cities, because the air is so thin, and there would not be enough oxygen to support fierce flames.

The underground railway, or 'metro', in Moscow carries over six-and-a-half million people every day.

A collector in New York has amassed a collection of 7780 *different* cigarettes.

The only Englishman ever to become Pope was Nicholas Breakspear, who became Pope Adrian IV in 1154.

Sharkfin soup is one of the most prized dishes in China and the Far East. It can take up to five days to prepare.

Acknowledgements

Photographs: Page 3 Heather Angel; 4 Keystone; 5 Franklin Berger Photography; 7 *top* Popperfoto, *bottom* National Portrait Gallery; 8 Zefa; 9 *middle* Welsh Tourist Board, *bottom* Zefa; 11 *top* Ironbridge Museum, *middle* Zefa, *bottom* John Wilkie; 12 Lego Ltd; 13 *top left* Canada House, *right* Mike Feeney; 14 Sandia Laboratories; 15 NASA; 16 Biofotos; 17 & 18 Pat Morris; 19 & 21 NHPA; 22 Z-Z Collection; 23 Tony Morrison; 25 Italian Trade Department; 26 *top* Shell UK Ltd, *bottom* Associated Press; 27 Hulton/Bettman; 28 *top* Mary Evans Picture Library, *bottom* Volkswagon GB Ltd; 29 Ford Motor Co; 30 J. Allan Cash; 33 *left, middle left & right* National Portrait Gallery, *right* French Institute Library, *bottom* Tate Gallery; 34 Guiness Books; 35 *top* Zefa, *bottom* Syndication International; 37 Popperfoto; 38 Gamma; 39 *top* Zefa, *bottom* Australian News and Information Bureau.

Picture Reasearch Penny J. Warn